Vocal/Piano

GREATEST POP/ROCK
VOCAL HARMONY SONGS

ISBN 978-1-5400-2955-3

For all works contained herein:
Unauthorized copying, arranging, adapting, recording, Internet posting, public performance,
or other distribution of the music in this publication is an infringement of copyright.
Infringers are liable under the law.

Visit Hal Leonard Online at
www.halleonard.com

Contact us:
Hal Leonard
7777 West Bluemound Road
Milwaukee, WI 53213
Email: info@halleonard.com

In Europe, contact:
Hal Leonard Europe Limited
42 Wigmore Street
Marylebone, London, W1U 2RN
Email: info@halleonardeurope.com

In Australia, contact:
Hal Leonard Australia Pty. Ltd.
4 Lentara Court
Cheltenham, Victoria, 3192 Australia
Email: info@halleonard.com.au

AFRICA

Words and Music by DAVID PAICH
and JEFF PORCARO

Copyright © 1982 Hudmar Publishing Co., Inc. and Rising Storm Music
All Rights for Hudmar Publishing Co., Inc. Controlled and Administered by Spirit Two Music, Inc.
All Rights Reserved   Used by Permission

The wild dogs cry out in the night ___ as they grow rest - less

long-ing for some sol - i - tar - y com - pa - ny. ___

(Ooh, ___ com - pa - ny.) ___

I know ___ that I ___ must do ___ what's right, ___ as sure as Kil - i - man - ja - ro

ris - es   like   O-lym - pus   a-bove the   Ser - en-get- i. _____

(Ooh, _____   Ser - en-get- i.) _____

I   seek __ to   cure __ what's   deep __ in - side,   fright-ened   of ___ this

thing that   I've __ be - come. __

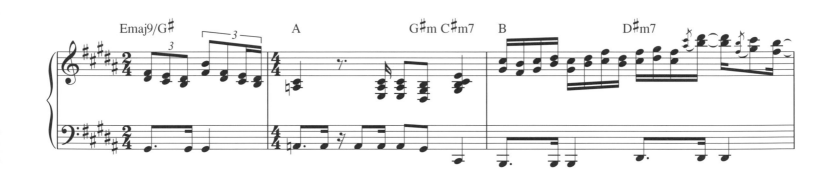

BOHEMIAN RHAPSODY

Words and Music by
FREDDIE MERCURY

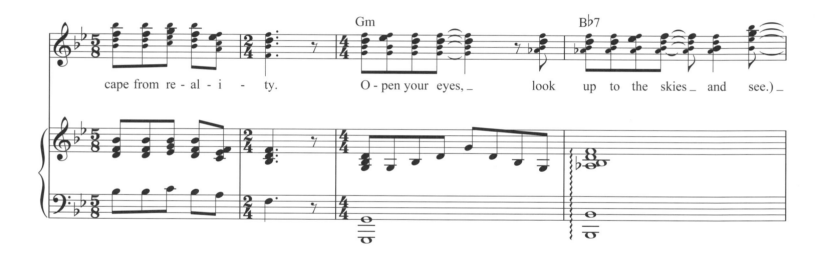

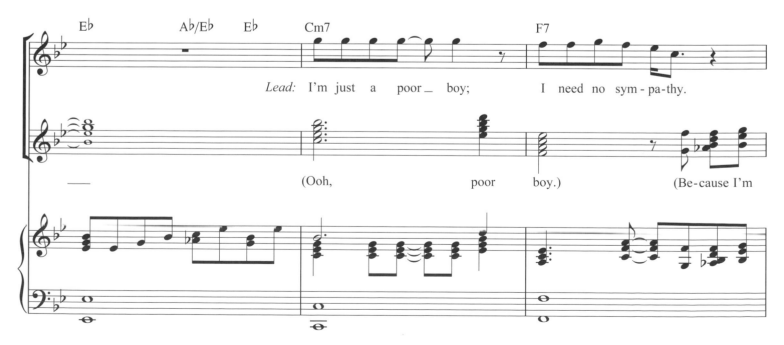

Copyright © 1975 Queen Music Ltd.
Copyright Renewed
All Rights Administered by Sony/ATV Music Publishing LLC, 424 Church Street, Suite 1200, Nashville, TN 37219
International Copyright Secured   All Rights Reserved

I'm not back a-gain__ this time to-mor - row, car-ry on, car-ry

D.S. al Coda

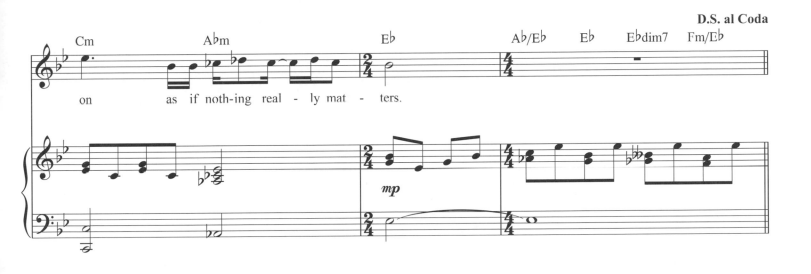

on as if noth-ing real - ly mat - ters.

CODA

Ma - ma,_____ ooh,_____ (An - y way the wind blows.)

(Ooh.)_____

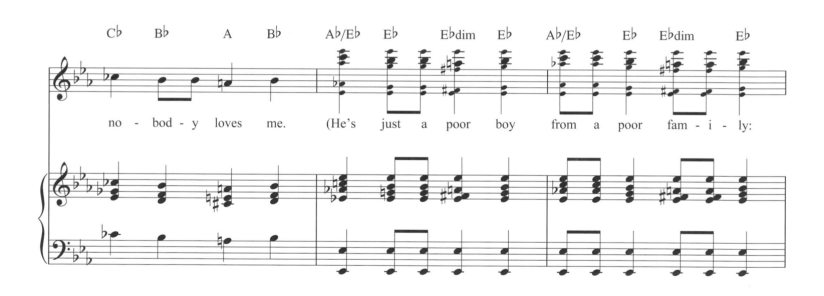

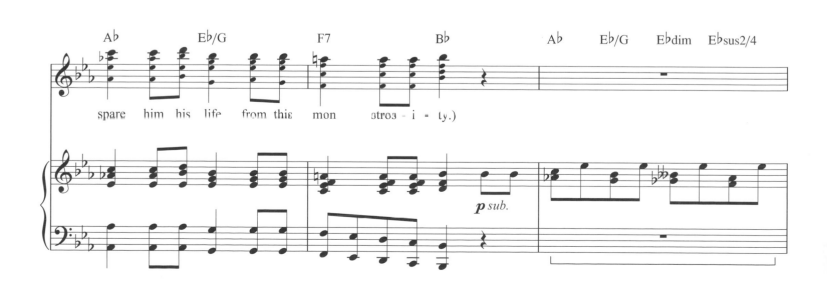

Heavy Shuffle

So ___ you think you ___ can stone me ___ and spit in my eye?

CALIFORNIA DREAMIN'

Words and Music by JOHN PHILLIPS
and MICHELLE PHILLIPS

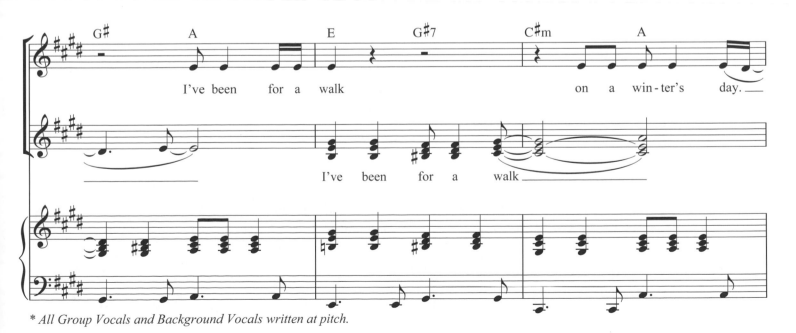

* *All Group Vocals and Background Vocals written at pitch.*

Copyright © 1965 UNIVERSAL MUSIC CORP.
Copyright Renewed
All Rights Reserved   Used by Permission

30

CARRY ON WAYWARD SON

Words and Music by
KERRY LIVGREN

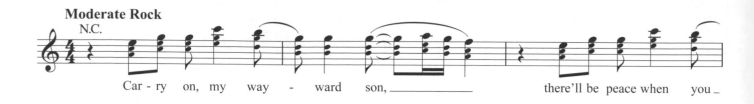

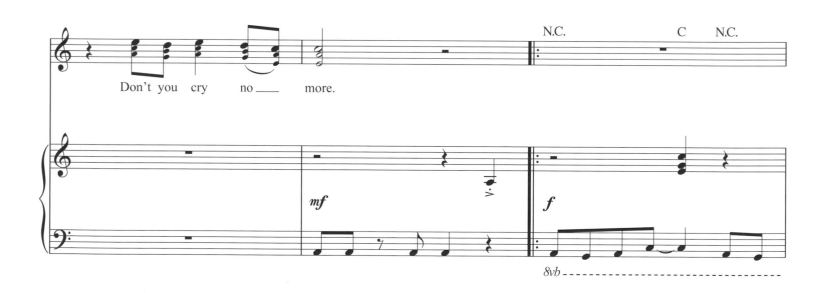

Copyright © 1976 EMI Blackwood Music Inc.
Copyright Renewed
All Rights Administered by Sony/ATV Music Publishing LLC, 424 Church Street, Suite 1200, Nashville, TN 37219
International Copyright Secured   All Rights Reserved

CODA

Don't you cry no ____ more." No!

Instrumental solo

Solo ends

8vb

GOOD VIBRATIONS

Words and Music by BRIAN WILSON
and MIKE LOVE

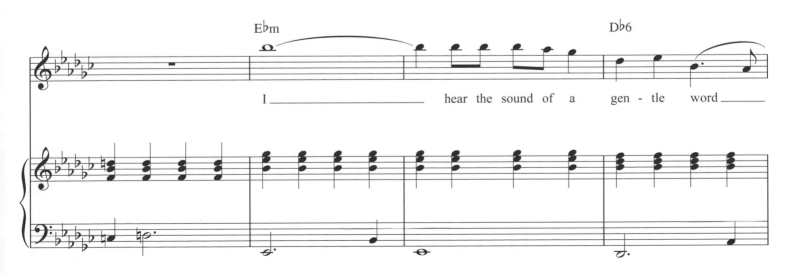

Copyright © 1966 IRVING MUSIC, INC.
Copyright Renewed
All Rights Reserved   Used by Permission

Solo III: & *Solo II:* Got - ta keep ___ those lov - in' good vi - bra - tions a hap-pen-in' with her. ___

* Got - ta keep ___ those lov - in' good vi - bra - tions a hap-pen - in' with her. ___

* Vocal fades out (next 4 meas.)

Ah.

Ah.

DANCING QUEEN

Words and Music by BENNY ANDERSSON,
BJÖRN ULVAEUS and STIG ANDERSON

Copyright © 1976, 1977 UNIVERSAL/UNION SONGS MUSIKFORLAG AB
Copyright Renewed
All Rights Administered by UNIVERSAL - POLYGRAM INTERNATIONAL PUBLISHING, INC. and EMI GROVE PARK MUSIC, INC.
All Rights Reserved   Used by Permission

you _ can jive, _____ hav - ing ____ the time of ____ your life. ____ Ooh, ooh,

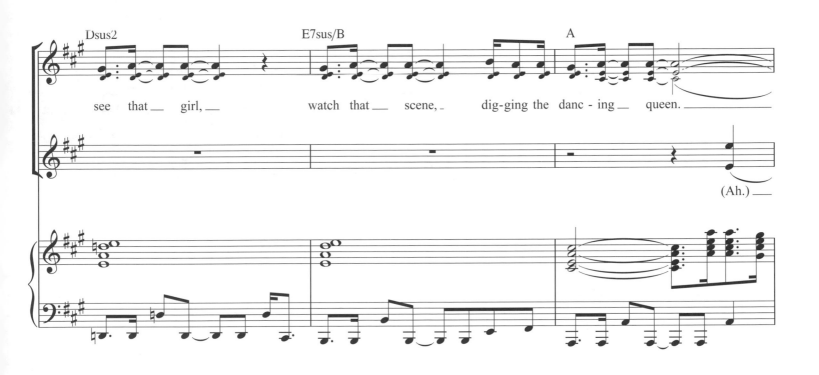

see that ____ girl, ____ watch that ____ scene, ____ dig-ging the danc - ing ____ queen. _____

(Ah.) ____

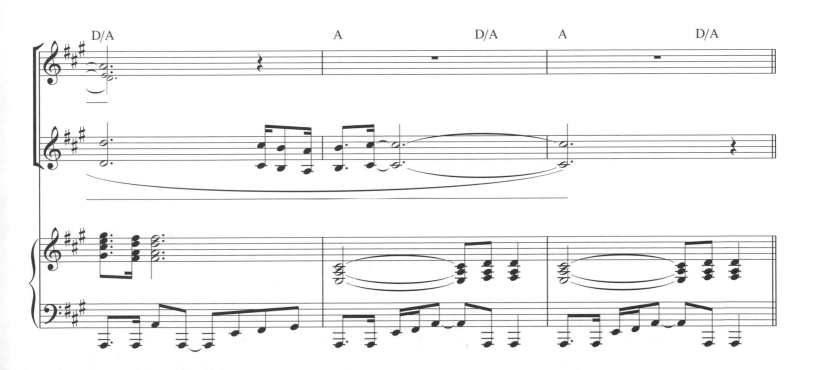

GO YOUR OWN WAY

Words and Music by
LINDSEY BUCKINGHAM

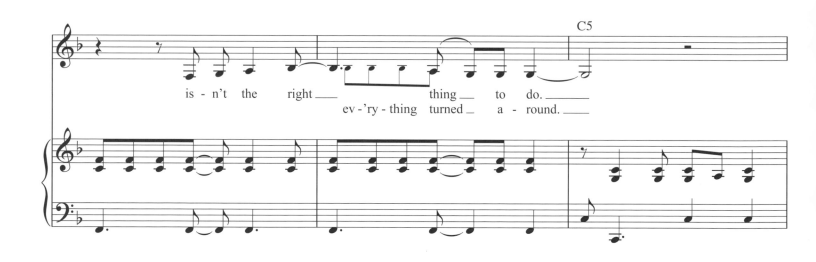

© 1976 (Renewed) NOW SOUNDS MUSIC
All Rights Administered by KOBALT SONGS MUSIC PUBLISHING
All Rights Reserved   Used by Permission

Solo ends

You can go ___
(You can go ___

I'VE SEEN ALL GOOD PEOPLE

Words and Music by JON ANDERSON
and CHRIS SQUIRE

Moderately fast Shuffle (♩ = 148)

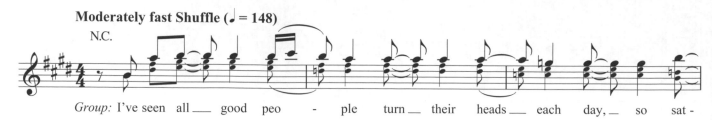

Slower (straight eighths) ♩ = 134

© 1971 (Renewed) TOPOGRAPHIC MUSIC LIMITED
All Rights Administered by WB MUSIC CORP.
All Rights Reserved   Used by Permission

in time with your time and ___ his news is cap - tured ___

___ *Lead:* for ___ the queen ___ to use.

Move me on ___ to an - y black square; ___ use me an - y - time ___

___ you ___ want. Just re - mem - ber that ___ the goal

Send an in - stant kar - ma to me; in - i - tial it

with lov - ing care, _____ your - self. _____

(Don't sur - round __ your - self.) _____

'Cause it's time, _ it's time in time with your time and _

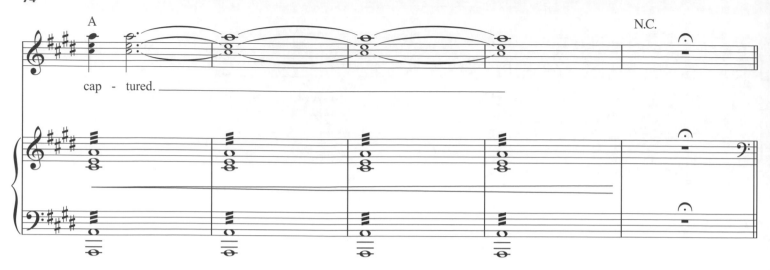

cap - tured. _____

Moderately fast Shuffle

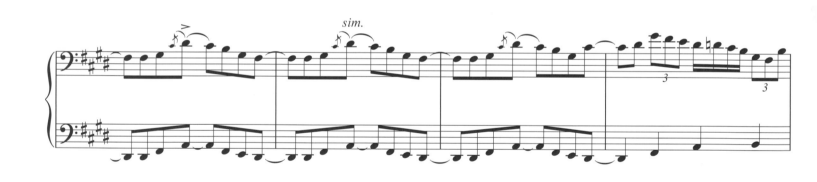

I've seen all ___ good peo - ple turn ___ their heads ___ each day, ___ so sat -

8vb

B7

E

I've seen all ___ good peo -

D/F#   C/G   G

- ple   turn ___ their   heads ___ each   day, ___ so   sat - is - fied, ___ I'm   on ___

A   C7/E

___ my   way. ___

I've seen all ___ good peo - ple turn ___ their heads ___

___ each day, ___ so sat - is - fied, ___ I'm on _____ my way. ___

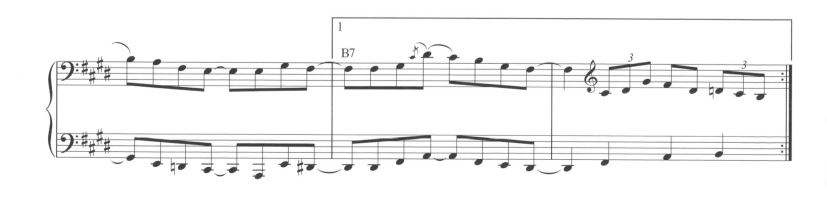

I've seen all ___ good peo - ple turn ___ their heads ___ each day, ___ so sat -

- is - fied, ___ I'm on ___ my way. ___ Yeah, yeah, ___

LISTEN TO THE MUSIC

Words and Music by
TOM JOHNSTON

© 1973 (Renewed) WARNER-TAMERLANE PUBLISHING CORP.
All Rights Reserved   Used by Permission

CODA

Lead: Like a la - zy flow - in' riv - er _____ sur - round - ing cas - tles in the sky. _ And the crowd is grow - ing big - ger, _____ lis - ten'n' for the hap - py sounds. _ and I got to let _ them fly. _

Group: Whoa _

whoa, _____ lis - ten to the mu - sic ___ all the time. _

Lis-ten to the mu - sic. Lis - ten to the mu - sic, babe. _

Repeat and Fade

Optional Ending

Whoa _

LYIN' EYES

Words and Music by DON HENLEY
and GLENN FREY

© 1975 (Renewed) CASS COUNTY MUSIC and RED CLOUD MUSIC
All Rights for CASS COUNTY MUSIC Administered by SONGS OF UNIVERSAL, INC.
Exclusive Print Rights Administered by ALFRED MUSIC
All Rights Reserved   Used by Permission

Harmony sung with lead vocal 1st time only.

†Vocal harmonies sung both times.

oth - er night ___ that's gon - na be ___ a long ___ one.

She draws the shade ___ and hangs ___ her head to cry. ___

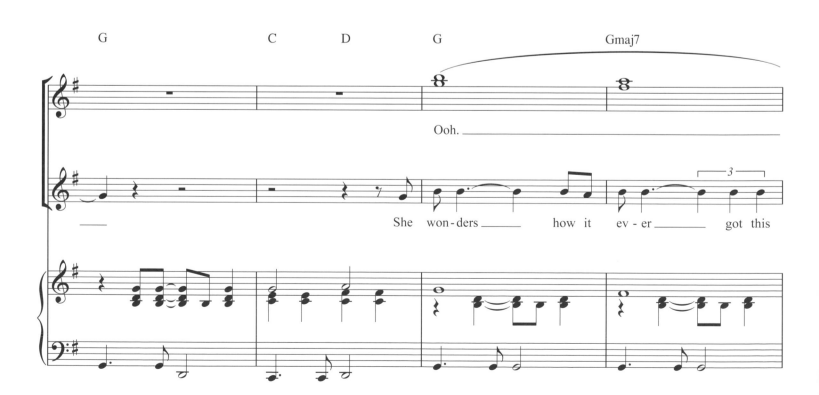

Ooh. ___

___ She won - ders ___ how it ev - er ___ got this

MR. BLUE SKY

Words and Music by
JEFF LYNNE

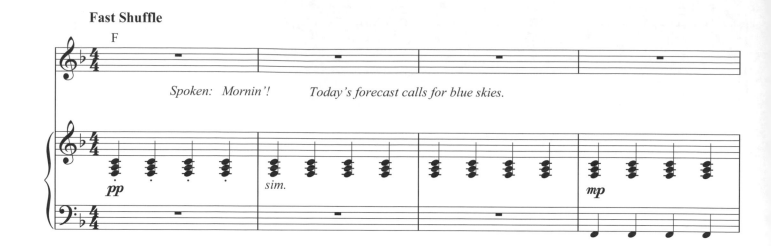

Spoken: Mornin'!   Today's forecast calls for blue skies.

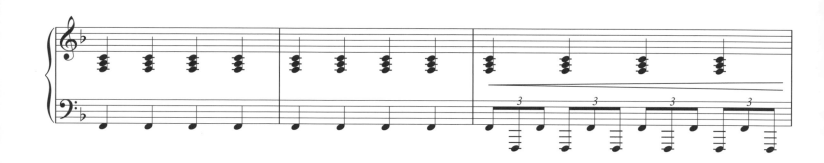

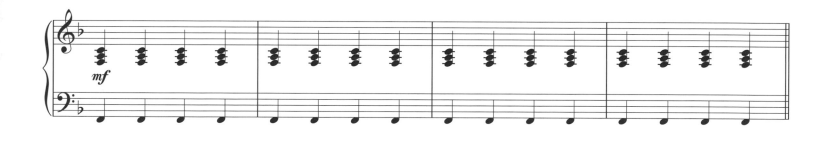

Lead: Sun is shin-ing in the sky;_____ there ain't_ a cloud_ in sight._

Copyright © 1978 EMI Blackwood Music Inc.
All Rights Administered by Sony/ATV Music Publishing LLC, 424 Church Street, Suite 1200, Nashville, TN 37219
International Copyright Secured   All Rights Reserved

116

MORE THAN A FEELING

Words and Music by
TOM SCHOLZ

Copyright © 1976 Pure Songs
Copyright Renewed
All Rights Administered by Next Decade Entertainment, Inc.
All Rights Reserved   Used by Permission

Instrumental solo

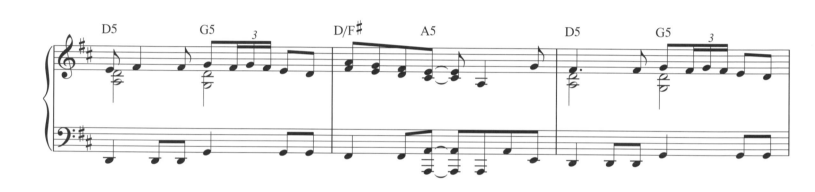

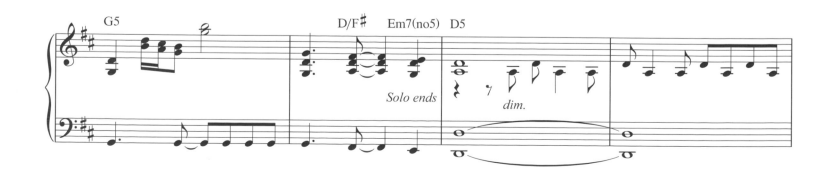

When I'm tired __ and think - ing cold, I hide in my mu - sic, for -

get the __ day, __ and dream of a girl __ I used to know. __ I

closed my __ eyes __ and she slipped a - way. __

NOWHERE MAN

Words and Music by JOHN LENNON
and PAUL McCARTNEY

Copyright © 1965 Sony/ATV Music Publishing LLC
Copyright Renewed
All Rights Administered by Sony/ATV Music Publishing LLC, 424 Church Street, Suite 1200, Nashville, TN 37219
International Copyright Secured   All Rights Reserved

SUITE: JUDY BLUE EYES

Words and Music by
STEPHEN STILLS

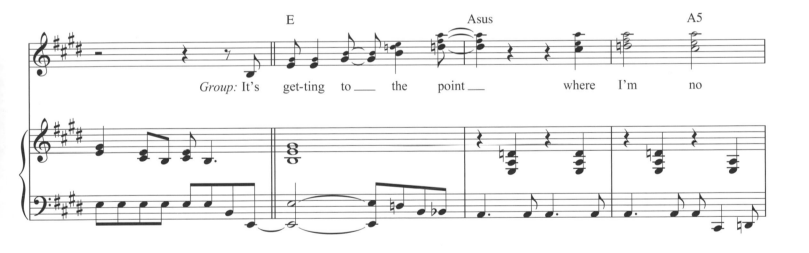

Group: It's get-ting to ___ the point ___ where I'm no

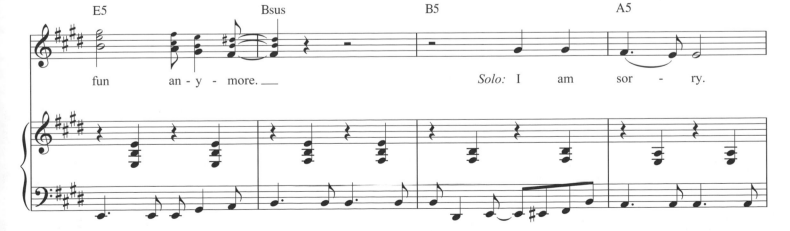

fun an-y-more. ___ Solo: I am sor-ry.

Copyright © 1970 Gold Hill Music, Inc.
Copyright Renewed
All Rights Reserved   Used by Permission

see _____ me _____ Thurs - days _____ and

Sat - ur - days? _____ Hey, hey, hey, what have you got to lose? _

Tempo I (Straight 4)

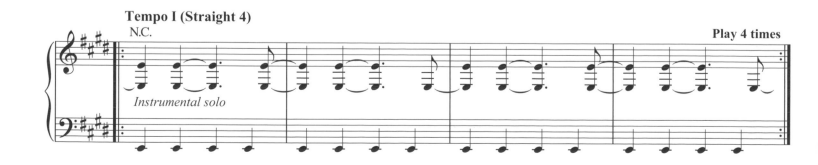

Instrumental solo

Play 4 times

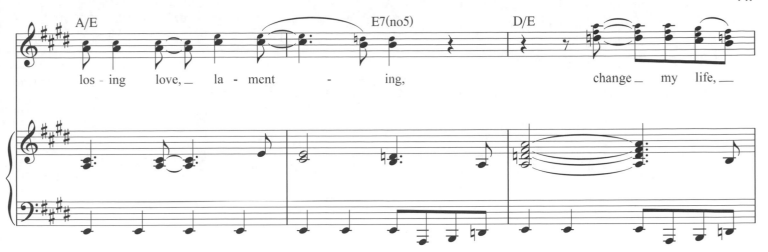

los-ing love, __ la - ment - ing, change __ my life, __

make __ it right, __ be my la - dy. _____

TOO MUCH HEAVEN

Words and Music by BARRY GIBB,
ROBIN GIBB and MAURICE GIBB

© 1978 UNICEF MUSIC
All Rights Administered by UNICHAPPELL MUSIC INC.
All Rights Reserved Used by Permission

Oh. _____ Ah, ah, _____ ah. _____

Repeat and Fade

Ah __ ah, __ ah. __

high as a moun - tain and hard - er to climb.) _____

Optional Ending

high as a moun - tain and hard - er to climb.) _____

UNCLE JOHN'S BAND

Words by ROBERT HUNTER
Music by JERRY GARCIA

Copyright © 1970 ICE NINE PUBLISHING CO., INC.
Copyright Renewed
All Rights Administered by UNIVERSAL MUSIC CORP.
All Rights Reserved   Used by Permission

YOU'RE THE INSPIRATION

Words and Music by PETER CETERA
and DAVID FOSTER

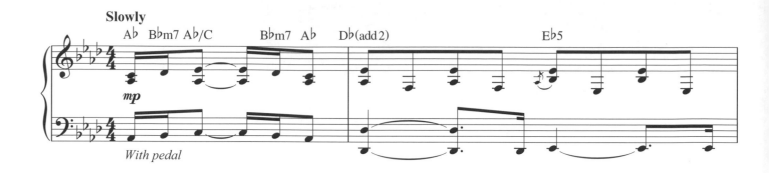

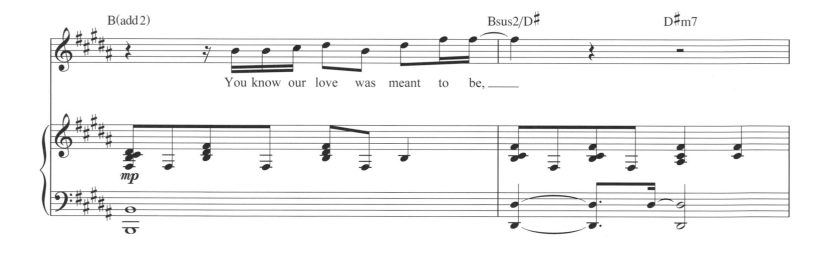

You know our love was meant to be,____

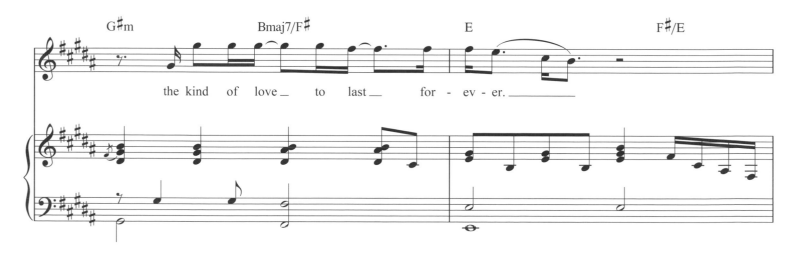

the kind of love _ to last _ for - ev - er. ____

Copyright © 1984 by Universal Music - MGB Songs and Peermusic III, Ltd.
International Copyright Secured   All Rights Reserved

THE WEIGHT

By J.R. ROBERTSON

Slowly, with a shuffle

With pedal

Lead: I pulled in - to Naz - a - reth; was feel-in' 'bout half past dead.

I just need some-place __ where I __ can lay __ my head. _____

"Hey, mis-ter, can you tell me where a man __ might find a bed?" __

Copyright © 1968, 1974 (Renewed) Dwarf Music
International Copyright Secured   All Rights Reserved
Reprinted by Permission of Music Sales Corporation

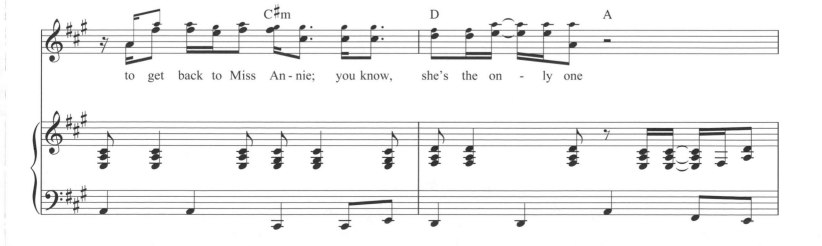